Poems about

Growth

Selected by
Amanda Earl & Danielle Sensier

Illustrated by
Frances Lloyd

Wayland

Titles in the series
Poems about . . .

Animals	**Food**
Colours	**Growth**
Day & Night	**Homes**
Families	**Journeys**
Feelings	**Weather**

For Viviane and Noël

Series editor: Catherine Baxter
Designer: Loraine Hayes

First published in 1995 by
Wayland (Publishers) Ltd
61 Western Road, Hove
East Sussex BN3 1JD, England

© Copyright 1995 Wayland
(Publishers) Ltd

Typeset by Dorchester Typesetting
Group Ltd., Dorset, England.
Printed and bound in Italy by
G. Canale & C.S.p.A., Turin.

British Library Cataloguing in Publication Data

Poems About Growth
   I. Earl, Amanda II. Sensier, Danielle
   808.81

   ISBN 0-7502-1126-1

Front cover design: S. Balley

Poets' nationalities

Aileen Fisher	American
Christina Rossetti	English/Italian
Kit Wright	English
Robert Fisher	American
Richard Edwards	English
Stanley Cook	English
Shel Silverstein	American
Danielle Sensier	English/Mauritian

Contents

A Spike of Green

When I went out
The sun was hot,
It shone upon
My flower pot.

And there I saw
A spike of green
That no one else
Had ever seen!

On other days
The things I see
Are mostly old
Except for me.

But this green spike
So new and small
Had never yet
Been seen at all!

Barbara Baker

4

The Seed

How does it know,
this little seed,
if it is to grow
to a flower or weed,
if it is to be
a vine or shoot,
or grow into a tree
with a long deep root?
A seed is so small
where do you suppose
it stores up all
of the things it knows?

Aileen Fisher

Spring Song

On the grassy banks
Lambkins at their pranks;
Woolly sisters, woolly brothers,
    Jumping off their feet,
While their woolly mothers
    Watch by them and bleat.

Christina Rossetti

The Sun

The sun is way up high,
shining in the sky.
The sun is very bright
and goes away at night.

The sun is hot.
It helps us a lot.
The sun sends out heat
to help us grow wheat.

Kathryn

Corn Song

Corn growing in the big field,
Cornrow in my hair,
Corn on granny's little toe,
Cornmeal in the air.

Pauline Stewart

from **Trees**

Trees are the kindest things I know,
They do no harm, they simply grow

And spread a shade for sleepy cows,
And gather birds among their boughs.

They give us fruit in leaves above,
And wood to make our houses of,

And leaves to burn on Hallowe'en
And in the Spring new buds of green.

Harry Behn

Acorn Haiku

Just a green olive
In its own little egg-cup:
It can feed the sky.

Kit Wright

From little acorns, great oak trees do grow.

Traditional British saying

Building a Skyscraper

They're building a skyscraper
Near our street.
Its height will be nearly
One thousand feet.

It covers completely
A city block.
They drilled its foundation
Through solid rock.

They made its framework
Of great steel beams
With riveted joints
And welded seams.

A swarm of workmen
Strain and strive,
Like busy bees
In a honeyed hive.

Building a skyscraper
Into the air
While crowds of people
Stand and stare.

Higher and higher
The tall towers rise
Like Jacob's ladder
Into the skies.

James S. Tippett

Fun fun fungi

Shhh! There is a secret in the woods
at autumn time
when leaves drip from the trees
and beads of dew hang like jewels
from spiders' webs
there is a secret in the woods
when cold winds
come whispering
fun fun fungi
from damp places
they rise and grow
toadstools
mushrooms
and fungi which cling and creep
along fallen logs
and in the hollows of trees
the fun fun fungi
of fairy rings

Robert Fisher

16

The Caterpillar

Brown and furry
Caterpillar in a hurry;
Take your walk
To the shady leaf or stalk.

May no toad spy you,
May the little bird pass by you;
Spin and die,
To live again a butterfly.

Christina Rossetti

Bramble Talk

A caterpillar on a leaf
Said sadly to another:
'So many pretty butterflies . . .

I wonder which one's Mother.'

Richard Edwards

18

Bluebells

This year and every year
The long-legged trees
Stand, now Spring is here,
In a bright blue sea.

No one can count the bluebells
That gather together
Until they fill
The woods with waves of their colour.

Beneath new shining leaves
On the long-legged trees
Children gather flowers
Paddle in a bluebell sea.

Stanley Cook

Magic Story of Falling Asleep

When the last giant came out of his cave
and his bones turned into the mountain
and his clothes turned into the flowers,

nothing was left but his tooth
which my dad took home in his truck
which my grandad carved into a bed

which my mum tucks me into at night
when I dream of the last giant
when I fall asleep on the mountain.

Nancy Willard

from **Me and My Giant**

I have a friend who is a giant,
And he lives where the tall weeds grow.
He's high as a mountain and wide as a barn,
And I only come up to his toe, you know,
     I only come up to his toe.

Shel Silverstein

23

I've Been Growing

Little by little, I've been growing,
It happened without me even knowing,
It happened so slowly without showing,
But today I *know* I've been growing.

For last year's coat which used to be roomy,
Today is tight and clinging to me,
It's short and it doesn't look right on the *new* me,
That's how I know I've been growing!

Daphne Lister

experiment

at school we're doing growing things
   with cress.
sprinkly seeds in plastic pots
   of cotton wool.

Kate's cress sits up on the sill
   she gives it water.
mine is shut inside the cupboard
   dark and dry.

now her pot has great big clumps
    of green
mine hasn't.
Mrs Martin calls it Science
    I call it mean.

Danielle Sensier

Amazonian Timbers, Inc.

This can go next –
here, let me draw the line.
That's roughly right,
give or take
a few square miles or so.
I'll list the ones we need.
No, burn the rest.

Only take the best,
we're not in this
for charity.
Replant? No –
you're new to this, I see!
There's plenty more
where that comes from,
no problem! Finish here –
and then move on.

Judith Nicholls

Yoruba Poem

Enjoy the earth gently
Enjoy the earth gently
For if the earth is spoiled
It cannot be repaired
Enjoy the earth gently

Anon

How to use this book

Poetry is a very enjoyable area of literature and children take to it naturally, usually beginning with nursery rhymes. It's what happens next that can make all the difference! This series of thematic poetry anthologies keeps poetry alive and enjoyable for young children.

When using these books there are several ways in which you can help a child to enjoy poetry and to understand the ways in which words can be carefully chosen and sculpted to convey different atmospheres and meanings. Try to encourage the following:

- Joining in when the poem is read out loud.
- Talking about favourite words, phrases or images.
- Discussing the illustration and photographs.
- Miming facial expressions to suit the mood of the poems.
- Acting out events in the poems.
- Copying out the words.
- Learning favourite poems by heart.
- Discussing the difference between a poem and a story.
- Clapping hands to rhythmic poems.
- Talking about metaphors/similes eg what kind of weather would a lion be? What colour would sadness be? What would it taste like? If you could hold it, how would it feel?

It is inevitable that, at some point, children will want to write poems themselves. Writing a poem is, however, only one way of enjoying poetry. With the above activities, children can be encouraged to appreciate and delight in this unique form of communication.

Picture acknowledgements

APM cover; Colorific 28/29 (J Kyle Keener/Matrix); Life File 24 (Nicola Sutton); Sally & Richard Greenhill 7; NHPA 12 (David Woodfall), 18 (G Bernard); Telegraph Colour Library 17 (Planet Earth/John Lythgoe); Tony Stone Worldwide 2 (Jo Browne/Mick Smee), 4/5 (Peter Correz), 8/9 (Mitch Kezar), 11 (Jo Browne/Mick Smee), 14/15 (Donovan Reese), 19 (Gay Bumgarner), 20/21 (Jane Gifford).

Text acknowledgements

For permission to reprint copyright material the publishers gratefully acknowledge the following: Edit Kroll Literary Agency for 'Me and My Giant' from *Where The Sidewalk Ends* by Shel Silverstein. Copyright © 1974 by Evil Eye Music Inc. Reprinted by permission of Edit Kroll Literary Agency; Faber & Faber for 'Amazonian Timbers Inc.' an extract from 'A Poem for the Rainforest' from *Midnight Forest/Magic Mirror* by Judith Nicholls. Reprinted by permission of the publisher; Aileen Fisher for 'The Seed'; Robert Fisher for 'Fun, Fun Fungi' from *Funny Folk* by Robert Fisher, published by Faber & Faber. Reprinted by permission of the author; Daphne Lister for 'I've Been Growing'; Sarah Matthews for 'Bluebells' from *The Squirrel In Town* by Stanley Cook. Copyright © Stanley Cook, published by Blackie. Reprinted by permission of Sarah Matthews; Orchard Books for 'Bramble Talk' from *A Mouse In My Roof* by Richard Edwards. Reprinted by permission of the publisher; Random House UK for 'Corn Song' from *Singing Down the Breadfruit* by Pauline Stewart; Nancy Willard c/o Jean V Naggar Literary Agency for 'Magic Story of Falling Asleep'. Reprinted by permission of the author. While every effort has been made to secure permission, in some cases it has proved impossible to trace the copyright holders. The publishers apologise for this apparent negligence.

Index of first lines